The Healthy Meal Prep Cookbook

Affordable Recipes for the Health-Conscious Cook.
Lose Weight Made Simple with 50 Family-Friendly
Meals Under 400 Calories

Amanda Altman

Table of Content:

the reader will render any resulting actions solely under their purview. There are no scenarios in which the publisher or the original author of this work can be in any fashion deemed liable for any hardship or damages that may befall them after undertaking information described herein.

Additionally, the information in the following pages is intended only for informational purposes and should thus be thought of as universal. As befitting its nature, it is presented without assurance regarding its prolonged validity or interim quality. Trademarks that are mentioned are done without written consent and can in no way be considered an endorsement from the trademark holder.

Introduction:

Thank you for choosing this guide. 50 Easy, Healthy Recipes to Lose Weight, With New Ideas and Tips You'll Love.

Luckily for you, this guide will help you get your life back to normal - starting with your diet!

Who would have thought your treatment could start right in your own kitchen?

With just a simple change in your diet to natural, healthy foods, you can prevent and treat a long list of medical conditions.

Take your health into your own hands - naturally!

1 - Shrimp Pasta		
Preparation	Cooking	Servings
50 min	**15 min**	**2**

Ingredients:

- 8 ounces linguine
- ¼ cup mayonnaise
- ¼ cup bean stew glue
- Two cloves garlic, squashes
- ½ pound shrimp, stripped

- One teaspoon salt
- ½ teaspoon cayenne pepper
- One teaspoon garlic powder
- One tablespoon vegetable oil
- One lime, squeezed
- ¼ cup green onion, slashed
- ¼ cup cilantro, minced
- Red bean stew chips, for embellish

Directions:

1. Cook pasta still somewhat firm as per box guidelines.
2. In a little bowl, consolidate mayonnaise, stew glue and garlic. Race to join.
3. Put in a safe spot.
4. In a blending bowl, include shrimp, salt, cayenne and garlic powder.
5. Mix to cover shrimp. Oil in a heavy skillet over medium warmth.
6. Include shrimp and cook for around 2 minutes at that point flip and cook for an extra 2 minutes.
7. Add pasta and sauce to the dish.
8. Mood killer the warmth and combine until the pasta is covered.

Nutrition: Calories: 283 Protein: 25 g Fat: 18 g Carbohydrates: 6g

2 - Chicken Thighs with Creamy Tomato Spinach Sauce

Preparation	Cooking	Servings
50 min	**10 min**	**2**

Ingredients:

- One tablespoon olive oil
- 1.5 lb. chicken thighs, boneless skinless
- ½ teaspoon salt
- ¼ teaspoon pepper
- 8 oz. tomato sauce
- Two garlic cloves, minced

- ½ cup overwhelming cream
- 4 oz. new spinach
- Four leaves fresh basil (or utilize ¼ teaspoon dried basil)

Directions:

1. The most effective method to cook boneless skinless chicken thighs in a skillet: In a much skillet heat olive oil on medium warmth.

2. Boneless chicken with salt and pepper.

3. Add top side down to the hot skillet. Cook for 5 minutes on medium heat, until the high side, is pleasantly burned.

4. Flip over to the opposite side and heat for five additional minutes on medium heat.

5. Expel the chicken from the skillet to a plate.

6. Step by step instructions to make creamy tomato basil sauce: To the equivalent, presently void skillet, include tomato sauce, minced garlic, substantial cream.

7. Bring to bubble and mix. Lessen warmth to low stew. Include new spinach and new basil.

8. Mix until spinach withers and diminishes in volume.

9. Taste the sauce and include progressively salt and pepper, if necessary.

10. Include back cooked boneless skinless chicken thighs, increment warmth to medium.

Nutrition: Calories: 106 Protein: 66g Fat: 77g Carbohydrates: 29g

3 - Prawn & Chili Pak Choi

Preparation	Cooking	Servings
30 min	30 min	2

Ingredients:

- 75g (2 ¼ oz.) brown rice
- 1 pak choi
- 60ml (2 fl. oz.) chicken stock
- 1 tbsp extra virgin olive oil
- 1 garlic clove, finely chopped
- 50g (1 ⅝ oz.) red onion, finely chopped

- ½ bird's eye chili, finely chopped
- 1 tsp freshly grated ginger
- 125g (4 ¼ oz.) shelled raw king prawns
- 1 tbsp soy sauce
- 1 tsp five-spice
- 1 tbsp freshly chopped flat-leaf parsley
- A pinch of salt and pepper

Directions:

1. Bring a medium sized saucepan of water to the boil and cook the brown rice for 25-30 minutes, or until softened.
2. Tear the pak choi into pieces.
3. Warm the chicken stock in a skillet over medium heat and toss in the pak choi, cooking until the pak choi has slightly wilted.
4. In another skillet, warm olive oil over high heat.
5. Toss in the ginger, chili, red onions and garlic frying for 2-3 minutes.
6. Throw in the prawns, five-spice and soy sauce and cook for 6-8 minutes, or until the cooked throughout.
7. Drain the brown rice and add to the skillet, stirring and cooking for 2-3 minutes.

8. Add the pak choi, garnish with parsley and serve.

Nutrition:Calories: 203 kcal Protein: 16g Fat: 15 g Carbohydrates: 50g

4 - Dahl with Kale, Red Onions and Buckwheat

Preparation	Cooking	Servings
10 min	**25 min**	**2**

Ingredients:

- 1 teaspoon of extra virgin olive oil
- 1 teaspoon of mustard seeds
- 40g (1 ½ oz.) red onions, finely chopped
- 1 clove of garlic, very finely chopped
- 1 teaspoon very finely chopped ginger
- 1 Thai chili, very finely chopped

- 1 teaspoon curry mixture
- 2 teaspoons turmeric
- 300ml (10 fl. oz.) vegetable broth
- 40g (1 ½ oz.) red lentils
- 50g (1 ⅝ oz.) kale, chopped
- 50ml (1.70 fl. oz.) coconut milk
- 50g (1 ⅝ oz.) buckwheat

Directions:

1. Heat oil in a pan at medium temperature and add mustard seeds. When they crack, add onion, garlic, ginger and chili. Heat until everything is soft.
2. Add the curry powder and 1 teaspoon of turmeric, mix well.
3. Add the lentils and cook them for 25 to 30 minutes until they are ready.
4. While the lentils are cooking, prepare the buckwheat.
5. Serve buckwheat and lentils.

Nutrition: Calories: 143 kcal Protein: 7.67 g Fat: 2.41 g Carbohydrates: 24.83 g

5 - Chickpeas, Onion, Tomato & Parsley Salad in a Jar

Preparation	Cooking	Servings
15 min	0 min	3

Ingredients:

- 1 cup cooked chickpeas
- ½ cup chopped tomatoes
- ½ of a small onion, chopped
- 1 tbsp. chia seeds
- 1 Tbsp. chopped parsley
- Dressing:

- 1 tbsp. olive oil and 1 tbsp. of Chlorella.
- 1 tbsp. fresh lemon juice and pinch of sea salt

Directions:

Put ingredients in this order: dressing, tomatoes, chickpeas, onions and parsley.

Nutrition: Calories: 210 Protein: 7g Fat: 9 g Carbohydrates: 26g

6 - Kale & Feta Salad with Cranberry Dressing

Preparation	Cooking	Servings
10 min	30 min	3

Ingredients:

- 9oz kale, finely chopped
- 2oz walnuts, chopped
- 3oz feta cheese, crumbled
- 1 apple, peeled, cored and sliced
- 4 medjool dates, chopped

For the Dressing:

- 3oz cranberries
- ½ red onion, chopped
- 3 tablespoons olive oil
- 3 tablespoons water
- 2 teaspoons honey
- 1 tablespoon red wine vinegar
- Sea salt

Directions:

1. Place the ingredients for the dressing into a food processor and process until smooth.

2. If it seems too thick you can add a little extra water if necessary.

3. Place all the ingredients for the salad into a bowl.

4. Pour on the dressing and toss the salad until it is well coated in the mixture.

Nutrition: Calories: 298 kcal Protein: 15 g Fat: 45g Carbohydrates: 70g

7 - Fried Chicken and Broccolini

Preparation	Cooking	Servings
15 min	**30 min**	**2**

Ingredients:

- 2 tablespoon Coconut oil

- 400 g (14 oz.) Chicken breast

- 150 g (5 ¼ oz.) Bacon cubes

- 250 g (8 oz.) Broccolini

Directions:

1. Cut the chicken into cubes.
2. Melt the coconut oil in a pan over medium heat and brown the chicken with the bacon cubes and cook through.
3. Season with chili flakes, salt and pepper.
4. Add broccolini and fry.
5. Stack on a plate and enjoy!

Nutrition: Calories: 361 Protein: 41 g Fat: 32g Carbohydrates: 4 g

8 - Frittata with Spring Onions and Asparagus

Preparation	Cooking	Servings
20 min	30 min	2

Ingredients:

- 5 pieces Egg
- 80 ml (3 fl. oz.) Almond milk
- 2 tablespoon Coconut oil
- 1 clove Garlic
- 100 g Asparagus tips
- 4 pieces Spring onions

- 1 teaspoon Tarragon
- 1 pinch Chili flakes

Directions:

1. Preheat the oven to 220°C (430°F).
2. Squeeze the garlic and finely chop the spring onions.
3. Whisk the eggs with the almond milk and season with salt and pepper.
4. Melt 1 tablespoon of coconut oil in a medium-sized cast iron pan and briefly fry the onion and garlic with the asparagus.
5. Remove the vegetables from the pan and melt the remaining coconut oil in the pan.
6. Pour in the egg mixture and half of the entire vegetable.
7. Place the pan in the oven for 15 minutes until the egg has solidified.
8. Then take the pan out of the oven and pour the rest of the egg with the vegetables into the pan.
9. Place the pan in the oven again for 15 minutes until the egg is nice and loose.
10. Sprinkle the tarragon and chili flakes on the dish before serving.

Nutrition: Calories: 398 Protein: 24g Fat: 37g Carbohydrates: 7g

9 - Cucumber Salad with Lime and Coriander

Preparation	Cooking	Servings
5 min	0 min	2

Ingredients:

- 1-piece Red onion
- 2 pieces Cucumber
- 2 pieces Lime (juice)
- 2 tablespoon fresh coriander

Directions:

1. Cut the onion into rings and thinly slice the cucumber. Chop the coriander finely.
2. Place the onion rings in a bowl and season with about half a tablespoon of salt.
3. Rub it in well and then fill the bowl with water.
4. Pour off the water and then rinse the onion rings thoroughly (in a sieve).
5. Put the cucumber slices together with onion, lime juice, coriander and olive oil in a salad bowl and stir everything well.
6. Refrigerator in a covered bowl for a few days.

Nutrition: Calories: 57 Protein: 2 g Fat: 0.41 g Carbohydrates: 13g

10 - Spinach and Turkey Lasagna

Preparation	Cooking	Servings
30 min	**30 min**	**4**

Ingredients:

- 9 whole-wheat lasagna noodles
- 1 teaspoon extra virgin olive oil
- ½ cup red onion, chopped
- 1-pound ground turkey breast
- 3 cups tomato sauce
- 1/2 cup mushrooms, sliced

- 1 teaspoon dried parsley
- 1 teaspoon dried lovage
- 1 teaspoon dried oregano
- ¼ teaspoon garlic powder
- Salt and pepper to taste
- 6 cups fresh spinach, chopped
- 2 cups ricotta cheese
- ¼ teaspoon ground nutmeg
- 2 cups shredded mozzarella cheese

Directions:

1. If you are trying to cut back on your dairy intake or if you simply find lasagna a bit too rich and cheesy for your preferences, try swapping the ricotta cheese for crumbled firm or medium firm tofu.
2. You will be adding another Sirtfood to the dish and it is much lighter, though surprisingly similar in taste and texture when covered with the sauce.
3. Preheat an oven to 375 degrees F.
4. Bring a large pot of lightly salted water to a boil.
5. Cook lasagna noodles until al dente, approximately 8 minutes.

6. Drain noodles and rinse under cold water.

7. Heat the olive oil in a skillet over medium heat.

8. Stir in the onion and cook until it softens and turns translucent, about 2 minutes.

9. Add ground turkey and cook 5 to 7 minutes more, stirring to break up any large chunks of meat.

10. Stir in tomato sauce, mushrooms, parsley, lovage, oregano, black pepper, and garlic powder.

11. Simmer for 2 minutes and season to taste.

12. Combine spinach, ricotta, and nutmeg in a large bowl.

13. To assemble, arrange 3 noodles lengthwise in the bottom of a greased 9x13 inch baking dish. Spread with 1/3 the spinach-ricotta mixture, 1/3 of the turkey mixture, and 1/3 of the mozzarella.

14. Repeat layers, ending with remaining mozzarella.

15. Bake in preheated oven for 25 minutes.

16. Cool for 5 minutes before serving.

Nutrition: Calories: 286 Protein: 23 g Fat: 9g Carbohydrates:31g

11 - Thai Curry with Chicken and Peanuts

Preparation	Cooking	Servings
20 min	**20 min**	**4**

Ingredients:

- 2 Bird's Eye chili peppers
- 2 tablespoons ginger root, chopped
- 1 tablespoon fresh turmeric root, chopped
- ½ teaspoon cumin
- ½ teaspoon dried coriander
- 1/2 teaspoon ground nutmeg

- 2 tablespoons lemongrass, thinly sliced
- 1 shallot, chopped
- 2 cloves garlic, chopped
- 2 teaspoons fermented shrimp paste
- 2 tablespoons fish sauce
- 3 tablespoons brown sugar
- 2/3-pound skinless, boneless chicken breast, cut into cubes
- 2 tablespoons extra virgin olive oil
- ½ cup roasted peanuts

Directions:

1. The mere scent of this dish will have your entire neighborhood clambering for a bowl of the heavenly curry.

2. Place the chili peppers in a bowl; pour enough water over the chili peppers to cover.

3. Allow the peppers to soak until softened, about 10 minutes. Drain, chop the peppers finely and set aside.

4. In a large bowl, add the ginger and turmeric root, cumin, coriander, lemongrass, shallot, garlic, shrimp paste, and chopped chili peppers and mash into a paste.

5. Stir the fish sauce and sugar into the paste.

6. Add the chicken to the paste and toss to coat the evenly.

7. Cover bowl and marinate for at least 20 minutes or up to 24 hours in the refrigerator.

8. Heat the oil in a large skillet over medium heat and cook the chicken until no longer pink in the center and the juices run clear, 5 to 7 minutes.

9. Stir 2 cups of water into the pan and add the peanuts.

10. Bring to a simmer and cook until thickened, 20 to 30 minutes.

11. You can also cook this at a lower temperature for up to 2 hours.

Nutrition: Calories: 396 Protein: 35 g Fat: 17 g Carbohydrates: 13g

12 - Red Lentil Curry

Preparation	Cooking	Servings
15 min	**25 min**	**4**

Ingredients:

- 2 cups whole red lentils
- 1 large red onion, diced
- 1 ½ tablespoons curry paste
- 2 tablespoons curry powder
- 1 teaspoon chili powder
- 1 teaspoon ground turmeric

- 1 teaspoon ground cumin
- 1 teaspoon salt
- 1 teaspoon sugar
- 3 cloves garlic, minced
- 1" section of fresh ginger root, peeled and minced
- 1 (14.25 ounce) can crushed tomatoes
- 1 tablespoon extra-virgin olive oil

Directions:

1. Lentils and curry are a match made in heaven.
2. The soft and creamy legumes soak up the curry sauce and ideal for pouring over rice or scooping up with fresh naan.
3. Rinse the lentils in a fine mesh sieve under cold water until the water runs clear - this will prevent your lentils from getting gummy.
4. Transfer the lentils to a medium-sized pot with enough water to cover completely and simmer covered until they are just starting to become tender, about 15 – 20 minutes. Add additional water, as necessary.
5. In the meantime, warm the oil in a large skillet and sauté the onions until they are golden.

6. In a separate bowl, combine the curry paste, curry powder, chili powder, turmeric, cumin, salt, sugar, garlic, and ginger and mix well.

7. When the onions are translucent, add the curry mixture and cook on high, stirring constantly for 2 - 3 minutes.

8. Add in the crushed tomato and reduce the heat. Let the curry blend simmer until the lentils are ready.

9. When the lentils are cooked to your liking, drain well, and add to the curry sauce, mixing well.

10. Serve immediately.

Nutrition: Calories: 257 Protein: 9 g Fat: 1 g Carbohydrates: 53g

13 - Spiced Fish Tacos with Fresh Corn Salsa

Preparation	Cooking	Servings
10 min	**20 min**	**4**

Ingredients:

- 1 cup corn
- 1/2 cup red onion, diced
- 1 cup jicama, peeled and chopped
- 1/2 cup red bell pepper, diced
- 1 cup fresh cilantro leaves, finely chopped
- 1 lime, zested and juiced

- 2 tablespoons sour cream
- 2 tablespoons cayenne pepper
- Salt and pepper to taste
- 8 (4 ounce) fillets tilapia
- 2 tablespoons olive oil
- 8 corn tortillas, warmed

Directions:

1. If you do not have any available, you can substitute for water chestnuts, celery, or radishes.
2. Preheat grill for high heat.
3. For the Corn Salsa: In a medium bowl, mix together corn, red onion, jicama, red bell pepper, and cilantro. Stir in lime juice and zest.
4. Brush each fillet with olive oil, and sprinkle with the cayenne and season to taste.
5. Arrange fillets on grill and cook for 3 minutes per side. For each fish taco, top two corn tortillas with fish, sour cream, and corn salsa.

Nutrition: Calories: 297 Protein: 25 g Fat: 1 g Carbohydrates: 23g

14 - Turkey Mole Tacos

Preparation	Cooking	Servings
10 min	20 min	3

Ingredients:

- Lean ground turkey - .75 pound
- Green onion, chopped – 4 stalks
- Garlic cloves, minced – 2
- Celery, chopped – 1 rib
- Roasted sweet peppers, chopped, and drained – 3.5 ounces

- Diced tomatoes, canned – 7 ounces
- Corn tortillas, 6 inches, warmed – 6
- Red onion, thinly sliced – 1
- Walnuts, roasted, chopped – 2 tablespoons
- Dark chocolate, chopped – 2 ounces
- Sea salt - .25 teaspoon
- Chili powder – 4 teaspoons
- Cumin - .5 teaspoon
- Cinnamon, ground - .125 teaspoon

Directions:

1. These tacos have a rich and deep flavor thanks to the mole, which is then complemented by the fresh red onion.

2. The meat is easily stored in the freezer until you plan to enjoy and assemble the tacos.

3. In a large skillet that is non-stick cook the ground turkey with the green onions, celery, and garlic over medium heat.

4. Cook until there is no pink remaining, the turkey has reached a temperature of one-hundred and sixty-five degrees, and the vegetables are tender.

5. Into the skillet with the cooked turkey add the canned tomatoes, roasted red peppers,

cinnamon, chocolate, chili powder, cumin, and sea salt.

6. Allow the liquid from the tomatoes to come to a boil before reducing the heat to medium-low, covering the skillet with a lid, and simmering for ten minutes.

7. Stir occasionally to prevent sticking and burning.

8. Remove the cooked ground turkey from the heat and stir in the walnuts.

9. Divide the taco meat between the corn tortillas, topping it off with the sliced red onion.

10. Serve while warm.

Nutrition: Calories: 369 Protein: 22 g Fiber: 6 g Carbohydrates:37g

15 - Artichoke & Eggplant Rice

Preparation	Cooking	Servings
10 min	10 min	3

Ingredients:

- 2 tablespoons olive oil
- 1 medium onion, finely chopped
- A handful parsley, chopped
- 1 teaspoon turmeric powder
- 3 cups vegetable stock
- Juice, lemon

- 1 eggplant, chopped into chunks
- 1 clove garlic, crushed
- 1 teaspoon smoked paprika
- 7 ounces paella rice
- 1 package chargrilled artichoke
- Lemon wedges to serve

Directions:

1. Place a nonstick pan or paella pan over medium heat. Add 1 tablespoon oil.
2. When the oil is heated, add eggplant and cook until brown all over.
3. Remove with a slotted spoon and place on a plate lined with paper towels.
4. Add 1 tablespoon oil.
5. When the oil is heated, add onion and sauté until translucent.
6. Stir in garlic and parsley stalks.
7. Cook for 10 minutes.
8. Add all the spices and rice and stir-fry for a few minutes until rice is well coated with the oil.
9. Add salt and mix well.
10. Pour half the broth and cook until dry.
11. Stir occasionally.

12. Add eggplant and artichokes and stir.

13. Pour remaining stock and cook until rice is tender.

14. Add parsley leaves and lemon juice and stir.

15. Serve hot with lemon wedges.

Nutrition: Calories: 361 Protein: 8 g Fat: 16 g Carbohydrates:54 g

16 - Sautee Tofu & Kale

Preparation	Cooking	Servings
15 min	15 min	3

Ingredients:

- 8 –12 oz. extra firm tofu
- 2 tbsps. olive oil
- ½ tsp. salt & pepper
- 1 tsp. garlic, minced
- 1 bunch kale, chopped

Directions:

- Heat oil in a large skillet over medium heat.
- Fry tofu in pan for 4-5 minutes.
- Add kale and stir fry for 3-4 minutes until kale is soft.
- Add salt, pepper and garlic, and cook for another 1-2 minutes until the garlic is fragrant.
- Drizzle sesame seeds on top.
- Serve and enjoy!

Nutrition: Calories: 206 Protein: 4 g Fat: 12 g Carbohydrates:14 g

17 - Baked Salmon Salad with Creamy Mint Dressing

Preparation	Cooking	Servings
15 min	**20 min**	**2**

Ingredients:

- 1 salmon fillet (130g)
- 40g mixed salad leaves
- 40g young spinach leaves
- 2 radishes, trimmed and thinly sliced
- 5cm piece (50g) cucumber, cut into chunks
- 2 spring onions, trimmed and sliced

- one small handful (10g) parsley, roughly chopped
- For the dressing
- 1 tsp low-fat mayonnaise
- 1 tbsp natural yoghurt
- 1 tbsp rice vinegar
- 2 leaves mint, finely chopped
- Salt to taste
- Freshly ground black pepper

Directions:

1. First, preheat your oven to 200°C
2. (180°C fan/Gas 6).
3. Now place the salmon fillet on a baking tray.
4. Bake it for 16–18 minutes until cooked.
5. Now remove it from the oven and set aside.
6. The salmon is equally useful to be you used as hot or cold in the salad.
7. If salmon has skin, simply cook skin side down. Remove the salmon from the skin.
8. It slides off easily when cooked.
9. Now mix the mayonnaise, yoghurt, rice wine vinegar, and the mint leaves.
10. Add salt and pepper.
11. Leave them to stand for at least 5 minutes.

12. It allows the

13. flavors to develop.

14. Arrange salad leaves and spinach on a serving plate. Top with the radishes, cucumber, the spring onions and parsley.

15. Now Flake the cooked salmon onto the salad.

16. Finally, drizzle the dressing over.

Nutrition: Calories: 306 Protein: 4 g Fat: 2 g Carbohydrates:1g

18 - Easy Peasy Chicken Curry

Preparation	Cooking	Servings
15 min	**30 min**	4

Ingredients:

- Three garlic cloves, roughly chopped
- One red onion, roughly chopped
- Two teaspoons of garam masala
- 2 cm fresh ginger, peeled and roughly chopped
- Two teaspoons of ground turmeric
- Two teaspoons of ground cumin

- One cinnamon stick, optional
- One tablespoon of olive oil
- Six cardamom pods, optional
- 1 x 400ml tinned coconut milk
- Eight boneless, skinless chicken thighs (or 4 chicken breasts), cut into bitesize chunks
- 200 gm of buckwheat brown rice or basmati rice to serve
- 2 tablespoons of fresh coriander chopped (plus extra for garnish)

Directions:

1. In the food processor, put the onion, garlic and ginger and process until it's a paste.
2. Alternatively, chop these three ingredients thoroughly and continue as below, if you don't have one.
3. Stir the garam masala into the paste with cumin and turmeric. Set aside.
4. Placed in a big, deep pan (ideally non-stick), 1 tablespoon of olive oil.
5. For a minute, heat up the bowl, then add the chopped chicken thighs.

6. Pour the chicken over a high heat, and add to the curry paste.

7. Turn it down for 2 minutes.

8. Let the chicken cook for 3 minutes in the paste and then add half the milk (200ml) and the cinnamon (if using) as well as the Cardamom.

9. Turn down and cook until the curried sauce is thick and delicious, and then let it simmer for 30 minutes.

10. Apply more coconut milk as the curry starts to heat. You may not need anything, but if you want a much cleverer curry, add the lot!

11. Make your accompaniment (snack / rice) and any side dishes during the cooking process.

12. When the curry is finished, add the sliced coriander and serve with sweet or rice and a good glass of white chilled wine or medium water immediately!

Nutrition: Calories: 275 Protein: 8 g Fat: 2 g Carbohydrates:31g

19 - Turmeric Chicken & Kale Salad with Honey, Lime Dressing

Preparation	Cooking	Servings
20 min	**10 min**	**2**

Ingredients:

- For the chicken
- 1 teaspoon ghee or 1 tbsp coconut oil
- ½ medium brown onion, diced
- 250-300 g / 9 oz. chicken mince or diced up chicken thighs
- 1 large garlic clove, finely diced

- 1 teaspoon turmeric powder
- 1teaspoon lime zest
- juice of ½ lime
- ½ teaspoon salt + pepper

For the salad

- Broccolini: 6 stalks or 2 cups of broccoli florets
- Pumpkin seeds (pepitas): 2 tablespoons
- 3 large Kale leaves, stems removed, chopped
- ½ Avocado, slices
- Handful of fresh coriander leaves, chopped
- Handful of fresh parsley leaves, chopped

For the dressing

- 3 tablespoons lime juice
- 1 small garlic clove, finely diced or grated
- tablespoons extra-virgin olive oil (I used 1 tablespoon avocado oil and * 2 tablespoons EVO)
- 1 teaspoon raw honey
- ½ teaspoon wholegrain or Dijon mustard
- ½ teaspoon sea salt and pepper

Directions:

1. First of all, heat the ghee or coconut oil in a small frying pan.
2. Keep heat medium to high.
3. Add onion and sauté on medium heat for 4-5 minutes, until they are golden.
4. Now add chicken mince and garlic and stir for 2 to3 minutes over medium to high.
5. Now add the turmeric, lime zest, lime juice, salt and pepper and cook them.
6. Stir frequently, for a further 3 to 4 minutes.
7. Set aside the cooked mince.
8. While the chicken is being cooked, bring a small saucepan of water to boil.
9. Add the broccolini in it and cook for 2 minutes.
10. Rinse under cold water and cut into 3 to 4 pieces each.
11. Now add the pumpkin seeds to frying pan from the chicken.
12. Toast over medium heat for 2 minutes.
13. Stir frequently to prevent burning.
14. Now Season with a little salt. Set it aside.
15. Raw pumpkin seeds are also fine to use.
16. Place the chopped kale in a salad bowl.
17. Pour the dressing over it. With your hands, toss and massage the kale with the dressing.

18. This will soften the kale, like what citrus juice does to the fish or beef carpaccio as it 'cooks' it lightly.
19. Finally toss it through the cooked chicken, broccolini, fresh herbs, pumpkin seeds and avocado slices.

Nutrition: Calories: 206 Cal Fat: 4g Carbohydrates: 10g Protein:10g

20 - Shrimp & Arugula Soup

Preparation	Cooking	Servings
10 min	30 min	3

Ingredients:

- 10 medium sized shrimp or 5 large prawns, cleaned, deshelled and deveined
- 1 small red onion, sliced very thinly
- 1 cup arugula
- 1 cup baby kale
- 2 large celery stalks, sliced very thinly

- 5 sprigs of parsley, chopped
- 11 cloves of garlic, minced
- 5 cups of chicken or fish or vegetable stock
- 1 tbsp extra virgin olive oil
- Dash of sea salt
- Dash of pepper

Directions:

1. Sauté the vegetables (not the kale or arugula just yet however), in a stock pot, on low heat for about 2 minutes so that they are still tender and still crunchy, but not cooked quite yet.
2. You will need to save the Cook time for the next step.
3. Add the salt and pepper.
4. Next, clean and chop the shrimp into bite-sized pieces that would be comfortable eating in a soup.
5. Then, add the shrimp to the pot, and sauté for 10 more minutes on medium-low heat.
6. Make sure the shrimp is cooked thoroughly and is not translucent.

7. When the shrimp seems to be cooked through, add the stock to the pot and cook on medium for about 20 more minutes.

8. Remove from heat and cool before serving.

Nutrition: Calories: 390 Carbs: 32g Fat: 27g Protein: 23g

21 - Chicken and Lentil Stew

Preparation	Cooking	Servings
10 min	40 min	3

Ingredients:

- 4 chicken breasts, diced
- ½ cup red lentils, rinsed
- 1 carrot, chopped
- 1 small onion, chopped
- 1 garlic clove, chopped
- 1 celery stalk, chopped

- 1 small red pepper, chopped
- 1 can tomatoes, chopped
- 1 tbsp paprika
- 1 tsp ginger, grated
- 3 tbsp extra virgin olive oil
- ½ cup fresh parsley leaves, finely cut, to serve

Directions:

1. Heat olive oil in a casserole and gently brown the chicken, stirring.
2. Add in onions, garlic, celery, carrot, pepper, paprika and ginger.
3. Cook, stirring constantly, for 2-3 minutes.
4. Add in the lentils and tomatoes and bring to a boil.
5. Lower heat, cover, and simmer for 30 minutes, or until the lentils are tender and the chicken is cooked through.
6. Serve sprinkled with fresh parsley.

Nutrition: Calories: 311 Carbs: 36g Fat: 4g Protein: 32g

22 - Salmon Kebabs

Preparation	Cooking	Servings
10 min	**15 min**	**3**

Ingredients:

- 2 shallots, ends trimmed, halved
- 2 zucchinis, cut in 2-inch cubes
- 1 cup cherry tomatoes
- 6 skinless salmon fillets, cut into 1-inch pieces
- 3 limes, cut into thin wedges

Directions:

1. Preheat a barbecue or char grill on medium-high.
2. Thread fish cubes onto skewers, then zucchinis, shallots and tomatoes.
3. Repeat to make 12 kebabs.
4. Bake the kebabs for about 3 minutes each side for medium cooked.
5. Move to a plate, cover with foil and set aside for 5 min to rest before serving.

Nutrition: Calories: 300 Carbs: 7g Fat: 16g Protein: 30 g

23 - Lemon Rosemary Fish Fillets

Preparation	Cooking	Servings
10 min	20 min	2

Ingredients:

- 4 white fish fillets
- 1 tbsp dried rosemary
- 4 tbsp breadcrumbs
- 2 tbsp lemon zest
- 1 tsp garlic powder
- 2 tbsp extra virgin olive oil

- 1 tsp salt

Directions:

1. Combine the rosemary, breadcrumbs, lemon zest, garlic powder and salt in a food processor and blend until well mixed.
2. Add the fish fillets, skin-side up, on a lined baking tray.
3. Grill for 3-4 minutes.
4. Turn the fish over and press a quarter of the breadcrumb mixture over the top of each fillet.
5. Drizzle with olive oil and grill for 4 min until the crust is golden and the fish is cooked through.
6. Serve with steamed spinach or baked potatoes.

Nutrition: Calories: 100 Carbs: 0g Fat: 3g Protein: 17g

24 - Asian Salmon with Broccoli

Preparation	Cooking	Servings
10 min	**10 min**	**2**

Ingredients:

- 4 salmon fillets, skin on
- 1 lb. fresh broccoli florets
- 2 tbsp soy sauce
- 2 tbsp toasted sesame oil
- 1 tsp chili garlic sauce
- 1 tbsp brown sugar

- ½ cup green onions, finely cut, to serve

Directions:

1. Combine the garlic and soy sauce with the sesame oil and brown sugar in a large bowl.
2. Add in the salmon and broccoli and toss to coat.
3. Place salmon skin side down in a single layer on a lined baking tray.
4. Add the broccoli florets around.
5. Bake 10-12 minutes or until the fish is cooked through and flakes easily with a fork.
6. Top with green onions and serve.

Nutrition: Calories: 256 Carbs: 8g Fat: 15g Protein: 23g

25 - Salmon and Spinach with Feta Cheese

Preparation	Cooking	Servings
5 min	15 min	2

Ingredients:

- 4 salmon fillets, skin on
- 1 bag frozen spinach
- 4-5 green onions, chopped
- 1 cup crumbled feta cheese
- 4 tbsp extra virgin olive oil
- Salt and pepper, to taste

- Lemon wedges, to serve

Directions:

1. In a skillet, heat olive oil on medium-high.
2. Cook the spinach and the green onions for 2-3 min, stirring once or twice.
3. Drizzle with salt and pepper to taste and add in the feta cheese.
4. Cook for 1 minute more.
5. Place salmon skin side down in a single layer on a lined baking tray and roast for 10-12 minutes or until it is cooked through and flakes easily with a fork.
6. Spoon the spinach mixture onto plates, then top with the salmon and serve with lemon wedges.

Nutrition: Calories: 250 Carbs: 2g Fat: 10g Protein: 31g

26 - Prawn Arrabbiata

Preparation	Cooking	Servings
10 min	**20 min**	**2**

Ingredients:

- 125-150 g Raw or cooked prawns (Ideally ruler prawns)
- 65 g Buckwheat pasta
- 1 tbsp. extra virgin olive oil
- For arrabbiata sauce
- 40 g Red onion, finely slashed
- 1 Garlic clove, finely slashed

- 30 g Celery, finely slashed
- 1 Bird's eye bean stew, finely hacked
- 1 tsp Dried blended herbs
- 1 tsp extra virgin olive oil
- 2tbsps. White wine (discretionary)
- 400 g Tinned slashed tomatoes
- 1 tbsp. Chopped parsley

Directions:

1. Fry the onion, garlic, celery and bean stew and dried herbs in the oil over a medium-low warmth for 1–2 minutes.
2. Turn the heat up to medium, include the wine and cook for one moment.
3. Include the tomatoes and leave the sauce to stew over a medium-low warmth for 20–30 minutes, until it has a pleasant creamy consistency.
4. On the off chance that you feel the sauce is getting too thick just include a little water.
5. While the sauce is cooking, carry a container of water to the bubble and cook the pasta as per the bundle guidelines.

6. At the point when prepared just as you would prefer, channel, hurl with the olive oil and keep in the container until required.

7. On the off that you are utilizing crude prawns mix them to the sauce and bake for a further 3–4 minutes until it has turned pink and dark, including the parsley and serve.

8. If you are utilizing cooked prawns, include them with the parsley, carry the sauce to the bubble and help.

9. Add pasta to the sauce, blend altogether yet tenderly and serve.

Nutrition: Calories:150 Carbohydrates: 2g Fat: 25g Protein:10g

27 - Perfect Cauliflower Mash

Preparation	Cooking	Servings
5 min	**10 min**	**4**

Ingredients:

- 1 large head cauliflower, cored and cut in large florets
- 1 cup low-sodium chicken broth
- 3 tablespoons unsalted butter
- ½ tablespoon garlic powder
- Salt to taste
- Pepper to taste

Directions:

1. Add the cauliflower and broth to the Instant Pot.

2. Lock the lid and set the Pressure Release to Sealing. Select the Pressure Cook or Manual setting and set the cooking time to 5 minutes at high pressure.

3. Once the timer goes off, use a kitchen towel or oven mitts to protect your hand and move the pressure release knob to venting to perform a quick pressure release.

4. Drain, reserving any excess broth, and return the cauliflower to the pot.

5. With a potato masher, immersion blender, or fork, mash to your desired consistency, adding broth as needed for more moisture.

6. Stir in the butter and garlic powder, and add salt and pepper to taste.

7. Note: For more flavor, mix in fresh herbs such as thyme or rosemary before serving.

8. You can also stir in a splash of unsweetened original almond milk for a creamier mash.

Nutrition: Calories: 141 Fat: 9.1g (sat 5.5g), Cholesterol: 22.6mg Protein: 5.6g Carbohydrate: 12.6g Fiber: 5.4g Sugar: 5.4g Sodium: 107 mg

28 - Balsamic Roasted Beets

Preparation	Cooking	Servings
5 min	**10 min**	**6**

Ingredients:

- 6 medium beets (about 2 in. in diameter), unpeeled
- 3 tablespoons balsamic vinegar
- 2 tablespoons olive oil
- Salt to taste
- Pepper to taste

Directions:

1. Wash the beets well and remove any leaves.

2. Add 1 cup of water to the Instant Pot and place the trivet on top.

3. Arrange the beets on the trivet.

4. Lock the lid and set the Pressure Release to Sealing. Select the Pressure Cook or Manual setting and set the cooking time to 10 minutes at high pressure.

5. Once the timer goes off, use a kitchen towel or oven mitts to protect your hand and move the Pressure Release knob to Venting to perform a quick pressure release.

6. Remove the beets, allow to cool, and peel. The skin should slip off easily. Slice the beets into rounds or chop them into bite-sized pieces. Dress them with the balsamic vinegar, olive oil, and salt and pepper to taste.

7. Serve immediately or allow to marinate for 30 minutes for more flavor.

Nutrition: Calories: 82.1 Cal Fat: 4.6g (sat 0.6g) Cholesterol: 0mg Protein: 1.4g Carbohydrate: 9.2g Fiber: 2.3g Sugar: 6.7g Sodium: 82mg

29 - Flavor Bomb Asian Brussels Sprouts

Preparation	Cooking	Servings
5 min	**6 min**	**4**

Ingredients:

- ¾ cup vegetable broth
- 3 tablespoons soy sauce
- 1 tablespoon rice wine vinegar
- 2 tablespoons sesame oil
- 2 teaspoons garlic powder
- 1 teaspoon onion powder

- 1 teaspoon paprika
- ¼ teaspoon cayenne pepper
- 1 tablespoon almonds, raw, chopped
- 2 lbs. Brussels sprouts, halved

Directions:

1. Preheat an air fryer to 400 degrees F (200 degrees C).

2. In a small bowl, combine the vegetable broth, soy sauce, rice wine vinegar, sesame oil, garlic powder, onion powder, paprika, cayenne pepper, and salt. Set aside.

3. Select the Sauté setting and add the almonds.

4. Stir constantly until toasted, watching them carefully so they don't burn.

5. Spoon almonds into a small bowl and set aside.

6. Press Cancel to turn off the Sauté setting then add the reserved sauce to the pot.

7. Add the brussels sprouts and stir well to coat them in the sauce.

8. Lock the lid and set the Pressure Release to Sealing. Select the Pressure Cook or Manual setting and set the cooking time to 1 minute at high pressure.

9. Once the timer goes off, use a kitchen towel or oven mitts to protect your hand and move the Pressure Release knob to Venting to perform a quick pressure release.

10. Open the lid and taste, adding salt and pepper to taste, if necessary.

11. Garnish with the toasted almonds and serve warm over cauliflower rice or as a side for a lean protein.

12. Note: For spicier brussels sprouts, try doubling or tripling the quantity of cayenne pepper, or add a few tablespoons of your favorite hot sauce.

Nutrition: Calories: 184 Cal Fat: 8.7g (sat 1.2g) Cholesterol: 0mg Protein: 9.2g Carbohydrate: 23.2g Fiber: 9.2g Sugar: 5.8g Sodium: 733 mg

30 - Grilled fish fillet with pesto sauce

Preparation	Cooking	Servings
15 min	10 min	4

Ingredients:

- 2 white fish fillets (200 g each)
- 1 tablespoon olive oil
- pepper & sal

Pesto Sauce:

- 1 bunch fresh basil

- 2 garlic cloves
- 1 tablespoon pine nuts
- 1 tablespoon grated Parmesan cheese
- 1 cup extra-virgin olive oil

Directions:

Heat the Philips Airfryer to 180C.

Brush the fish fillets with the oil and season with pepper & salt.

Place in the cooking basket of the Airfryer and slide the basket into the Philips Airfryer.

Set the timer for 8 minutes.

Pick the basil leaves and place them with the garlic, pine nuts, Parmesan cheese and olive oil in a food processor or pestle and mortar.

Pulse or grind the mixture until it turns into a sauce. Add some salt to taste.

Place the fish fillets on a serving plate and serve them drizzled with the pesto sauce.

Nutrition: 402 calories; protein 43.3g; carbohydrates 3.1g; fat 123.5g; cholesterol 58.3mg; sodium 1773.2mg.

31 - Sweet Potato Hash

Preparation	Cooking	Servings
15 min	20 min	6

Ingredients:

- 2 large sweet potato, cut into small cubes
- 2 slices bacon, cut into small pieces
- 2 tablespoons olive oil
- 1 tablespoon smoked paprika
- 1 teaspoon sea salt
- 1 teaspoon ground black pepper

- 1 teaspoon dried dill weed

Directions:

1. Preheat an air fryer to 400 degrees F (200 degrees C).

2. Toss sweet potato, bacon, olive oil, paprika, salt, pepper, and dill in a large bowl.

3. Place mixture into the preheated air fryer.

4. Cook for 12 to 16 minutes.

5. Check and stir after 10 minutes and then every 3 minutes until crispy and browned.

Nutrition: 191 calories; protein 3.7g; carbohydrates 31.4g; fat 6g; cholesterol 3.3mg; sodium 446.8mg.

32 - Roasted Sweet Potatoes

Preparation	Cooking	Servings
5 min	**8 min**	**4**

Ingredients:

- ¼ cup olive oil
- 4 medium sweet potatoes (about 1 ¼ lbs. total), peeled or unpeeled, in 1-inch pieces
- 1 teaspoon garlic powder
- 1 teaspoon sea salt
- ¼ teaspoon pepper

- 1 cup chicken low-sodium broth

Directions:

1. Select the Sauté setting on the Instant Pot and heat the olive oil or butter.
2. Add the sweet potatoes, salt, pepper, and garlic powder to the pot and sauté for 5 minutes, stirring constantly. Add the broth and stir well.
3. Press Cancel to reset the cooking method.
4. Lock the lid and set the Pressure Release to Sealing. Select the Pressure Cook or Manual setting and set the cooking time to 7 minutes at high pressure.
5. Once the timer goes off, use a kitchen towel or oven mitts to protect your hand and move the Pressure Release knob to Venting to perform a quick pressure release.
6. Open the lid and taste, adding salt and pepper to taste, if necessary. Serve warm over a salad or as a side for chicken or another protein.
7. Note: This recipe can be adapted many ways, according to your family's tastes. Try adding a favorite spice mix, curry powder, or cayenne pepper before pressure cooking, fresh herbs like

rosemary and thyme after cooking, or a drizzle of truffle oil before serving.

Nutrition: Nutrition: Calories: 243 Cal Fat: 13.9g (sat 2g) Cholesterol: 0mg Protein: 3.4g Carbohydrate: 27.5g total Fiber: 4g Sugar: 5.7g Sodium: 671 mg

33 - **Simplest Brothy Beans**

Preparation	Cooking	Servings
5 min	**35 min**	**4**

Ingredients:

- 1 lb. dried white beans, such as great northern, cannellini, or chickpeas
- 1 medium yellow onion, quartered
- 2 celery stalks, cut in half
- 1 medium carrot, peeled and cut in half
- 8 cups water

- Salt to taste
- Freshly ground pepper to taste
- Extra virgin olive oil to taste
- 1 lemon, juiced

Directions:

1. In the Instant Pot, add the beans, onion, celery, carrots, water, and 1 teaspoon of salt.
2. Lock the lid and set the Pressure Release to Sealing. Select the Pressure Cook or Manual setting and set the cooking time to 35 minutes at high pressure.
3. Once the timer goes off, let sit for at least 10 minutes; the pressure will release naturally.
4. Then switch the Pressure Release to Venting to allow any last steam out.
5. Open the Instant Pot and season beans generously with salt and pepper, tasting the broth as you add seasoning until it's to your taste.
6. Serve warm, drizzled with a few drops of olive oil and lemon juice.

Nutrition: Nutrition: Calories: 399 Cal Fat: 1.7g (sat 0.4g) Cholesterol: 0mg Protein: 24.2g Carbohydrate: 74.4g Fiber: 29.1g Sugar: 2.3g Sodium: 622mg

34 - Southern Stewed Greens

Preparation	Cooking	Servings
12 min	**5 min**	**4**

Ingredient:

- ¼ lb. bacon, in 1-inch pieces
- 5 cloves garlic, roughly chopped
- 2 large bunches collard greens (about 4 cups), de-stemmed and roughly chopped
- 3/4 cup low-sodium chicken broth
- Salt to taste

- Pepper to taste
- Optional: 1 tablespoon apple cider vinegar

Directions:

1. Select the Sauté setting and add the bacon, cooking until it has rendered its fat and crisped up, 5-7 minutes. Add the garlic and cook, stirring constantly, for 1 minute.

2. Add the greens, broth, and salt and pepper to taste. You may need to add the greens in batches, stir, and allow to wilt slightly until it all fits in the pot.

3. Press Cancel to reset the cooking method.

4. Lock the lid and set the Pressure Release to Sealing. Select the Pressure Cook or Manual setting and set the cooking time to 5 minutes at high pressure.

5. Once the timer goes off, use a kitchen towel or oven mitts to protect your hand and move the Pressure Release knob to Venting to perform a quick pressure release.

6. Open the lid, taste, and add more salt and pepper if necessary.

7. If desired, stir in 1 tablespoon of apple cider vinegar to add brightness to the dish.

8. Serve warm.

Nutrition: 263 calories; protein 40.2g; carbohydrates 0.3g; fat 10.1g; cholesterol 86.2mg; sodium 913.1mg.

35 - Avocado Toast

Preparation	Cooking	Servings
12 min	**12 min**	**2**

Ingredients:

- ¼ cup all-purpose flour
- ½ teaspoon ground black pepper
- ¼ teaspoon salt
- 1 egg
- 1 teaspoon water

- 1 ripe avocado, halved, seeded, peeled and cut into 8 slices
- ½ cup panko bread crumbs
- cooking spray

Directions:

1. Preheat air fryer to 400 degrees F (200 degrees C).

2. Mix flour, pepper, and salt together in a shallow bowl. Beat together egg and water in a second shallow bowl. Place panko in a third shallow bowl.

3. Dredge an avocado slice through the flour, shaking off excess. Dip into egg and allow excess to drop off. Finally press slice into panko so both sides are covered. Set on a plate and repeat with the remaining slices.

4. Spray avocado slices generously with cooking spray and arrange in the bowl of the air fryer, sprayed-side down. Spray the top side of the avocado slices as well.

5. Cook in the preheated air fryer for 4 minutes. Turn avocado slices over and cook until golden, about 3 more minutes.

Nutrition:Calories: 30 Fat: 2g Calcium: 58g Protein: 2g

36 - Beef with A Red Wine

Preparation	Cooking	Servings
5 min	**30 min**	**3**

Ingredients:

- 100g potatoes, stripped and cut into 2cm bones
- 1 tbsp additional virgin olive oil
- 5g parsley, finely slashed
- 50g red onion, cut into rings
- 50g kale, cut
- 40ml red wine

- 1 tsp corn flour, broke down in 1 tbsp water

Directions:

1. Warmth the stove to 220°C/gas 7.
2. Spot the potatoes in a pot of bubbling water, take back to the bubble and cook for 4–5 minutes, at that point channel.
3. The spot in a broiling tin with one teaspoon of the oil and dish in the hot grill for 35–45 minutes.
4. Turn the potatoes at regular intervals to guarantee in any event, cooking.
5. At the point when cooked, expel from the stove, sprinkle with the hacked parsley.
6. Fry the onion in 1 tbsp of the oil medium warmth for 5–7 minutes, until delicate and pleasantly caramelized. Keep warm.
7. Steam the kale for 2–3 minutes at that point channel. Fry the garlic delicately in ½ teaspoon of oil for one moment, until delicate however not hued.
8. Include the kale and fry for a further 1–2 minutes, until careful. Keep warm.
9. Warmth an ovenproof skillet over heat until smoking. Coat the meat in ½ a tsp of the oil and

fry in the hot container over a medium-high warmth as indicated by how you like your meat done.

10. If you want your meat medium, it is smarter to burn the flesh and afterwards move the skillet to a grill set at 220°C/gas seven and finish the cooking that path for the endorsed occasions.

11. Include the stock and tomato purée to the steak skillet and bring to the bubble, at that point add the corn flour glue to thicken your sauce, including it a little at once until you have your ideal consistency.

12. Mix in any of the juices from the refreshed steak and present with the simmered potatoes, kale, onion rings and red wine sauce.

Nutrition: Calories: 280 Fat: 2g Calcium: 18g Potassium: 2g

37 - Beef Tenderloin

Preparation	Cooking	Servings
8 min	**30 min**	**8**

Ingredients:

- 2 pounds beef tenderloin, at room temperature
- 1 tablespoon vegetable oil
- 1 teaspoon dried oregano
- 1 teaspoon salt
- ½ teaspoon cracked black pepper

Directions:

1. Preheat the air fryer to 400 degrees F (200 degrees C). Pat beef tenderloin dry with paper towels.

2. Place tenderloin on a plate. Drizzle oil all over the beef and sprinkle with oregano, salt, and pepper. Rub spices and oil into the meat. Place the roast in the air fryer basket by folding it to make it fit. Close the basket.

3. Reduce heat to 390 degrees F (198 degrees C). Air fry for 22 minutes. Reduce heat again to 360 degrees F (182 degrees C). Cook for 10 minutes more. An instant-read thermometer inserted into the center should read 135 degrees F (57 degrees C) for medium.

4. Remove tenderloin from the basket and place on a plate. Allow to rest, uncovered, for at least 10 minutes before serving.

Nutrition: 235 calories; protein 32.4g; carbohydrates 0.2g; fat 10.6g; cholesterol 89.6mg; sodium 357.7mg.

38 - Chicken Pram Lasagna

Preparation	Cooking	Servings
5 min	30 min	4

Ingredients:

- Three chicken bosoms
- salt, to taste
- pepper, to taste
- 1 cup generally useful flour (125 g)
- Five eggs, separated
- 2 cups Italian bread pieces (230 g)

- vegetable oil, for broiling
- 2 cups ricotta cheddar
- 24 Oz marinara sauce (680 g)
- ½ cups destroyed mozzarella cheddar
- ½ cups destroyed parmesan cheddar
- new basil, to embellish

Directions:

1. Cut chicken bosoms down the middle (pound slim if fundamental) and season with salt and pepper.

2. Include the flour, four eggs, and bread morsels to 3 separate shallow dishes.

3. Beat the eggs.

4. Coat the chicken in the flour, at that point the eggs, lastly in the bread scraps.

5. Fry the chicken on the two sides until brilliant darker, around 4 minutes on each side.

6. Let channel on paper towels.

7. In a medium bowl, join the ricotta cheddar and the rest of the egg.

8. Preheat the grill too (180°C). Spread about ⅓ of the marinara sauce over the base of a goulash dish.

9. Rehash to make another layer, at that point finish with the rest of the sauce and mozzarella and Parmesan cheeses.

10. Appreciate!

Nutrition:Calories: 268 Fat: 5g Magnesium: 55g Potassium: 32g

39 - Sesame Chicken Salad

Preparation	Cooking	Servings
5 min	30 min	4

Ingredients:

- 1 tbsp sesame seeds
- One cucumber, stripped, split lengthways, deseeded with a teaspoon and cut
- 100g child kale, generally cleaved
- 60g pak choi, finely destroyed
- ½ red onion, finely cut

- Huge bunch (20g) parsley, cleaved
- 150g cooked chicken, destroyed

For the dressing:

- 1 tbsp additional virgin olive oil
- 1 tsp sesame oil
- Juice of 1 lime
- 1 tsp clear nectar
- 2 tsp soy sauce

Directions:

1. Toast the sesame seeds in a dry grill for 2 minutes until delicately cooked and fragrant. Move to a plate to cool.
2. In a little bowl, combine the olive oil, sesame oil, lime juice, nectar and soy sauce to make the dressing.
3. Place the cucumber, kale, pak choi, red-onion and parsley in a considerable bowl and tenderly combine. Pour over the dressing and blend once more.
4. Distribute the serving of mixed greens between two plates and top with the destroyed chicken.

Nutrition:Calories:168 Fat:5g Sodium: 25g Magnesium:69g

40 - Lemon Chicken Soup

Preparation	Cooking	Servings
12 min	12 min	4

Ingredients:

- 1 tablespoon olive oil
- 1 medium onion, chopped
- 3 cloves garlic, roughly chopped
- 2 medium carrots, peeled and sliced
- 6 stalks celery, sliced
- 8 cups fat-free chicken broth

- 1 teaspoon dried thyme
- Salt to taste
- Pepper to taste
- 1½ lbs. boneless skinless chicken breasts
- 4 oz. whole wheat spaghetti, broken in 1-inch pieces
- 1 bunch kale, stemmed and roughly chopped, to yield 1.5 cups
- 2 lemons, juiced
- Optional: lemon wedges for serving

Directions:

1. Select the Sauté setting and heat the olive oil.
2. Add the onion, garlic, carrots, and celery and sauté for 4-6 minutes. Add the chicken broth and thyme.
3. Taste and add salt and pepper to taste.
4. Add the chicken breasts and stir well.
5. Press Cancel to reset the cooking method.
6. Lock the lid and set the Pressure Release to Sealing. Select the Soup setting and set the cooking time to 6 minutes at high pressure.
7. Once the timer goes off, let sit for at least 10 minutes; the pressure will release naturally.
8. Then switch the Pressure Release to Venting to allow any last steam out.

9. Open the Instant Pot and remove the chicken and shred.

10. Add the broken spaghetti and stir; cook for time indicated on package.

11. Add the chicken back to the pot and stir in the kale and lemon juice.

12. Ladle into bowls and serve with an extra squeeze of lemon, drizzle of olive oil, or fresh cracked pepper.

Nutrition:Calories:378 Fat:7g Protein:45g Cabohydrates:5g

41 - Buttermilk Chicken

Preparation	Cooking	Servings
20 min	30 min	4

Ingredients:

- 1 cup buttermilk
- ½ teaspoon hot sauce
- ⅓ cup tapioca flour
- ½ teaspoon garlic salt
- ⅛ teaspoon ground black pepper
- 1 egg
- ½ cup all-purpose flour

- 2 teaspoons salt
- 1 ½ teaspoons brown sugar
- 1 teaspoon garlic powder
- ½ teaspoon paprika
- ½ teaspoon onion powder
- ¼ teaspoon oregano
- ¼ teaspoon black pepper
- 1 pound skinless, boneless chicken thighs

Directions:

1. Combine buttermilk and hot sauce in a shallow dish; mix to combine.

2. Combine tapioca flour, garlic salt, and 1/8 teaspoon black pepper in a resealable plastic bag and shake to combine.

3. Beat egg in a shallow bowl.

4. Mix flour, salt, brown sugar, garlic powder, paprika, onion powder, oregano, and 1/4 teaspoon black pepper in a gallon-sized resealable bag and shake to combine.

5. Dip chicken thighs into the prepared ingredients in the following order: buttermilk mixture,

tapioca mixture, egg, and flour mixture, shaking off excess after each dipping.

6. Preheat an air fryer to 380 degrees F (190 degrees C). Line the air fryer basket with parchment paper.

7. Place coated chicken thighs in batches into the air fryer basket and fry for 10 minutes. Turn chicken thighs and fry until chicken is no longer pink in the center and the juices run clear, an additional 10 minutes.

Nutrition: 335 calories; protein 24.3g; carbohydrates 27.4g; fat 13.6g; cholesterol 113.8mg; sodium 1549.8mg.

42 - Artichoke Hearts

Preparation	Cooking	Servings
15 min	**10 min**	**4**

Ingredients:

- 1 (14 ounce) can quartered artichoke hearts in water, drained
- 2 teaspoons grated Parmesan cheese
- ¼ teaspoon Italian seasoning
- ¼ teaspoon salt
- ⅛ teaspoon ground black pepper

- ⅛ teaspoon garlic powder
- 1 tablespoon olive oil

Directions:

1. Preheat the air fryer to 390 degrees F (200 degrees C).

2. Pat artichoke hearts dry with a paper towel to remove excess moisture and place in a bowl.

3. Sprinkle with Parmesan cheese, Italian seasoning, salt, pepper, and garlic powder.

4. Drizzle with olive oil and toss to coat.

5. Place in the air fryer basket and cook for 4 minutes. Shake basket and continue cooking until artichokes begin to brown and edges are crispy, 3 to 4 minutes more.

6. Serve immediately.

Nutrition: 167 calories; protein 2.6g; carbohydrates 6.6g; fat 3.7g; cholesterol 0.9mg; sodium 525.8mg.

43 - Moroccan Lentil Soup

Preparation	Cooking	Servings
12 min	30 min	4

Ingredients:

- 1 tablespoon olive oil
- 1 small onion, chopped
- 3 cloves garlic, minced
- 3/4 lb. ground turkey
- 1 tablespoon cumin
- 1 teaspoon garlic powder

- 1 teaspoon chili powder
- 1 teaspoon salt, plus more to taste
- ¼ teaspoon cinnamon
- Pepper to taste
- 5 cups beef broth
- 1 cup green or brown lentils

Directions:

1. Select the Sauté setting and heat the olive oil.
2. Add the onion and garlic and sauté until fragrant, 2-3 minutes.
3. Add the ground beef and cumin, garlic powder, chili powder, salt, cinnamon, and pepper.
4. Cook until very well-browned and beginning to sear. Add the beef broth and scrape up any browned bits from the bottom of the pot.
5. Add the lentils and stir well.
6. Press Cancel to reset the cooking method.
7. Lock the lid and set the Pressure Release to Sealing. Select the Soup setting and set the cooking time to 10 minutes at high pressure.
8. Once the timer goes off, let sit for at least 10 minutes; the pressure will release naturally.

9. Then switch the Pressure Release to Venting to allow any last steam out.

10. Open the Instant Pot and taste; add more salt and pepper to taste.

11. Ladle into bowls and serve with a drizzle of olive oil or fresh cracked pepper.

Nutrition:Calories:326 Fat:12g Protein:31g Cabohydrates:15g

44 - Sesame Chicken Thighs

Preparation	Cooking	Servings
7 min	**20 min**	**4**

Ingredients:

- 2 tablespoons sesame oil
- 2 tablespoons soy sauce
- 1 tablespoon honey
- 1 tablespoon sriracha sauce
- 1 teaspoon rice vinegar
- 2 pounds chicken thighs

- 1 green onion, chopped
- 2 tablespoons toasted sesame seeds

Directions:

1. Combine sesame oil, soy sauce, honey, sriracha, and vinegar in a large bowl.

2. Add chicken and stir to combine.

3. Cover and refrigerate for at least 30 minutes.

4. Preheat an air fryer to 400 degrees F (200 degrees C). Drain marinade from the chicken.

5. Place chicken thighs skin-side up in the basket of the air fryer. Cook for 5 minutes.

6. Flip and cook an additional 10 minutes.

7. Transfer chicken to a plate and let rest 5 minutes before serving.

8. Garnish with green onion and sesame seeds.

Nutrition: 385 calories; protein 39.5g; carbohydrates 6.6g; fat 32.6g; cholesterol 141.4mg; sodium 738.7mg.

45 – Light and Fresh Mediterranean Cod

Preparation	Cooking	Servings
10 min	15 min	6

Ingredients:

- 1 tablespoon butter
- 1 lemon, juiced
- 1 medium onion, sliced
- ½ teaspoon salt
- ½ teaspoon black pepper
- 1 teaspoon dried oregano

- 1-28 oz. can white beans
- 1 cup low-sodium chicken broth
- 2 tablespoons capers, drained,
- 6 cod fillets, about 8 oz. each

Directions:

1. Select the Sauté setting and heat the butter.
2. Add the remaining ingredients, except for the cod. Cook the sauce for 10 minutes.
3. Place the cod fillets in the sauce and spoon sauce over each fillet.
4. Press Cancel to reset the cooking method.
5. Lock the lid and set the Pressure Release to Sealing. Select the Steam setting and set the cooking time to 3 minutes at high pressure.
6. Once the timer has gone off and with a kitchen towel or oven mitts protecting your hand, move the Pressure Release knob to Venting to perform a quick pressure release.
7. Open the lid and taste the sauce, adding more salt and pepper if necessary.
8. Serve the cod with the beans and Mediterranean sauce.

Nutrition:Calories:372 Fat:4g Protein:31g Cabohydrates:5g

46 - Citrus Shrimp

Preparation	Cooking	Servings
5 min	**4 min**	**4**

Ingredients:

- 1 tablespoon butter
- 4 garlic cloves, minced
- ½ cup orange juice (100% pure, no sugar added)
- ½ cup low-sodium chicken broth
- 2 pounds of peeled and deveined raw shrimp
- 2 tablespoons lemon juice

- 1 teaspoon salt
- Pepper to taste

Directions:

1. Select the Sauté setting and heat the butter.
2. Add the garlic and cook until fragrant, 1-2 minutes. Add the orange juice and chicken broth.
3. Press Cancel to reset the cooking method, add the shrimp, and season with ½ teaspoon salt.
4. Lock the lid and set the Pressure Release to Sealing. Select the Steam setting and set the cooking time to 1 minute at high pressure.
5. Once the timer has gone off and with a kitchen towel or oven mitts protecting your hand, move the Pressure Release knob to Venting to perform a quick pressure release.
6. Open the lid and stir in lemon juice and adjust salt and pepper to taste.
7. Serve over white or brown rice, cauliflower rice, or mixed vegetables.

Nutrition:Calories:272 Fat:7g Protein:7g Cabohydrates:3g

47 - Pork Ragu

Preparation	Cooking	Servings
10 min	50 min	4

Ingredients:

- 18 oz. pork tenderloin
- 1 teaspoon salt
- Pepper to taste
- 1 tablespoon olive oil
- 6 garlic cloves
- 1-28 oz. can crush tomatoes, with juices

- 2 teaspoons dried thyme
- 1 teaspoon dried oregano
- Optional: 2 bay leaves

Directions:

1. Season the pork loin with salt and pepper.
2. Select the Sauté setting on the Instant Pot and heat the olive oil.
3. Add the pork loin to the Instant Pot and sear on all sides until browned.
4. Add the garlic, crushed tomatoes, thyme, oregano, and if using, bay leaves.
5. Lock the lid and set the Pressure Release to Sealing. Select the Meat/Stew setting and set the cooking time to 45 minutes at high pressure.
6. Once the timer goes off, let sit for at least 10 minutes; the pressure will release naturally.
7. Then switch the Pressure Release to Venting to allow any last steam out.
8. Open the lid and taste, adding more salt and pepper if necessary.
9. Shred the pork and serve over your favorite low-carb pasta, spaghetti squash, or spooned over vegetable fritters.

Nutrition:Calories:223 Fat:8g   Protein:10g Cabohydrates:8g

48 - Salmon with Turmeric and Chili

Preparation	Cooking	Servings
15 min	30 min	4

Ingredients:

- Skinned salmon
- 1 tsp. extra virgin olive oil
- 1 tsp. Ground turmeric
- 1/4 juice of a lemon
- 40 g red onion, finely chopped
- 60 g tinned green lentils

- 1 garlic clove, finely chopped
- 1 bird's eye chili, finely chopped
- 150 g celery cut into 2cm lengths
- 1 tsp. Mild curry powder
- 130 g tomato, cut into 8 wedges
- 100 ml chicken or vegetable stock
- 1 tbsp. Chopped parsley

Directions:

1. Heat the oven to 200c / gas mark 6.
2. Start with the spicy celery.
3. Heat a frying pan over a medium–low heat; add the olive oil, then the onion, garlic, ginger, chili, and celery. Fry gently for 2–3 minutes or until softened but not colored, then add the curry powder and cook for another minute.
4. Add the tomatoes, then the stock and lentils, and simmer gently for 10 minutes.
5. You may want to increase or decrease the cooking time depending on how crunchy you like your celery.
6. Meanwhile, mix the turmeric, oil, and lemon juice and rub over the salmon.

7. Place on a baking tray and cook for 8–10 minutes.

8. To finish, stir the parsley through the celery and serve with the salmon.

Nutrition:Calories:372 Fat:1g Protein:37g Cabohydrates:3gFiber:3

49 - Roasted Cauliflower

Preparation	Cooking	Servings
15 min	**20 min**	**2**

Ingredients:

- 3 cloves garlic
- 1 tablespoon peanut oil
- ½ teaspoon salt
- ½ teaspoon smoked paprika
- 4 cups cauliflower florets

Directions:

1. Preheat an air fryer to 400 degrees F (200 degrees C).

2. Cut garlic in half and smash with the blade of a knife. Place in a bowl with oil, salt, and paprika. Add cauliflower and turn to coat.

3. Place the coated cauliflower in the bowl of the air fryer and cook to desired crispiness, shaking every 5 minutes, about 15 minutes total.

4. After 15 minutes, the cauliflower will still have some crunch; cook for an additional 5 minutes if you want it softer. The timing really depends on the size of the cauliflower, so check frequently.

Nutrition: 118 calories; protein 4.3g; carbohydrates 12.4g; fat 7g; sodium 642.3mg.

50 - Chard and Sweet Potato Stew

Preparation	Cooking	Servings
15 min	**20 min**	**2**

Ingredients:

- 2 tablespoons olive oil
- 1 teaspoon cumin seeds, or 1 teaspoon ground cumin
- 1 medium onion, diced
- 2 medium sweet potatoes, peeled and in ½ inch cubes
- ½ teaspoon turmeric
- 1 tablespoon fresh ginger, peeled and minced

- 1 teaspoon salt
- 1 teaspoon ground coriander
- 2 cups vegetable broth
- 1 bunch Swiss chard (about 12 oz)
- Optional: lemon wedges for serving

Directions:

1. Select the Sauté setting and heat the olive oil. Add the onion and cook until translucent, 3-5 minutes.
2. If using cumin seeds, add them now and toast them for 1-3 minutes, until fragrant.
3. Otherwise, add the ground cumin in the next step.
4. Add the sweet potato, ground cumin (if using), ginger, turmeric, coriander, and salt and cook for 3-4 minutes. Add the vegetable broth and chard.
5. Taste and add more salt and pepper if needed.
6. Press Cancel to reset the cooking method.
7. Lock the lid and set the Pressure Release to Sealing. Select the Pressure Cook or Manual setting and set the cooking time to 8 minutes at high pressure.

8. Once the timer goes off, let sit for at least 10 minutes; the pressure will release naturally.

9. Then switch the Pressure Release to Venting to allow any last steam out.

10. Ladle into bowls and serve warm with a squeeze of lemon juice, if desired.

Nutrition: Calories:308 Fat:14g Protein:45g Cabohydrates:8g

THANK YOU

First of all, thank you for purchasing The Healthy Meal Prep
Cookbook

I know you could have picked any number of books to read,
but you chose this book, and for that, I am extremely grateful.

I hope that it added value and quality to your everyday life.

I wish you all the best in your future success!

Amanda Altman

CPSIA information can be obtained
at www.ICGtesting.com
Printed in the USA
BVHW041421260221
601200BV00005B/305

9 781954 474208